Florence & Isabelle in France

by Sylvia Rosemary Ann Kegg

Copyright @2020

All rights reserved

Published by Generous Heart

ISBN 978-1-9162572-4-5

Printed in United Kingdom

Cover design and interior layout by Loulita Gill Design

Illustrations by Tom Coombs

Photos kindly provided by Peter Kegg

Dedication

Sylvia wrote this book in 2011 for her amazing grandchildren, when she was suffering from Motor Neurone Disease, so that they would have something to remember her by.

The Macmillan Unit at Christchurch Hospital is a Specialist Palliative Care Unit and Hospice for patients in South East Dorset and South West Hampshire. The charity, Macmillan Caring Locally, works in partnership with the Royal Bournemouth and Christchurch Hospitals NHS Foundation Trust to provide the services at the Macmillan Unit and in the local community.

The unit is supported and funded by Macmillan Caring Locally providing an exceptional standard of care and a homely environment for patients, their families and visitors.

The charity also provides nursing and medical equipment to improve patient treatment and comfort. Macmillan Caring Locally is a small, community charity and is not connected in any way to the national charity Macmillan Cancer Support.

Sylvia was grandmother to 8 grandchildren. After Sylvia was diagnosed with Motor Neurone Disease she loved the support of the Macmillan Sisters and the time she spent in the Macmillan Unit in Christchurch, as the staff were exceptionally loving and caring.

All this book's profits, when the book is purchased, will go to Macmillan Caring Locally for their great work in end of life support.

Neal Williams
Trust Secretary
Christchurch Hospital
BH23 2JX
Registered charity No: 268218

For more information about Macmillan Caring Locally,
please visit www.macmillanlocal.org

Home

Florence and Isabelle were sisters. There was over a year's difference in their ages, but everyone thought they were twins. They had blond hair, were almost the same height and were both the same weight.

They lived with their parents in a big house in the country in France. It was a beautiful place for adventures. They had a vast garden with a large field and plenty of trees to climb and hide in.

Their Daddy was a carpenter and joiner, which meant he was good at making things with wood, especially furniture. He built the girls a lovely tree-house in one of the more significant trees in the front garden. It could not be seen from the road.

They spent many hours in it pretending to be pirates on the high seas, spying out the land and looking for any undesirables that might be lurking about the area. Sometimes they just sat there and read books.

A Special Place

There was always something exciting happening, like the day Daddy brought home an old caravan that a friend had given him for the children. Florence and Isabelle were really thrilled with it because it meant they had another place to play in, especially if it was raining and they couldn't play outside. Daddy covered the caravan with a camouflage tarpaulin so that it was more difficult to see from the house.

It blended in very well with the trees. They could have friends to stay and have a 'sleep-over' in the summer months. It was much more exciting to stay in the caravan with friends than in the house.

Near the caravan were some old pig-sheds that hadn't been used for a long time for pigs, and gradually over the years, Daddy had converted them for other uses. He had made one into a log store for their fires in the winter.

Another one he had made into a room to house all the machinery for the swimming pool which was in the garden. And another one was made into a playroom for Florence and Isabelle.

The girls had lots of places to play, which was really good because they lived such a long way from anywhere. There was never any problem of them getting bored, with so much to do where they were.

Making Memories

Mummy was a chef and made terrific food every day, although the girls didn't always appreciate just how good it was! Friends, family and neighbours asked Mummy to prepare meals and cakes for them for special occasions. She was always in demand by someone to do cooking or baking. In the garden Mummy and Daddy planted a large selection of vegetables so there were always fresh vegetables to have, as well as all the fruit from the plum trees, apple trees, fig-trees, pear trees, peach trees and many other varieties.

On one side of the house, Daddy had built a large hen-house for the chickens they had bought when they'd first moved into the house. These provided them with all the eggs they needed, and there were always some spares for friends and neighbours who came visiting. Every morning when Daddy opened the hen-house door, the girls would go in and collect the eggs that the chickens had laid.

One day the chickens refused to go back into the hen-house in the evening. Everyone was so surprised because they had always gone in straight away when Daddy called them. 'Maybe there is a lion or some other animal that's frightened them,' said Isabelle, who had a vivid imagination. 'Don't be silly,' said Florence. 'We don't have lions in this country, only in zoos.'

After investigating, Daddy discovered a snake's nest underneath the hen-house. 'That's why they are so afraid,' said Mummy. 'How are we going to get the chickens back in?' asked Florence, who was quite worried about losing any of them.

'They can't stay outside all night; otherwise a fox might come and eat them.' It was a difficult decision to make but, after securing the fence around the field, it was decided to leave the chickens outside and hope and pray that a fox wouldn't come.

The next morning Florence and Isabelle were up early to see if the chickens were safe, and found them all up in the trees. Everyone laughed because no-one had seen chickens in trees before.

Lilly & Woody

Then there was Lilly the pig. Lilly was a Vietnamese black pot-bellied pig. When Mummy and Daddy first brought her home, she was a small, cute little animal. The girls fell in love with this unusual pet.

She sat on everyone's lap and loved having the attention. As soon as anyone sat down, Lilly would plonk herself on them. When she was still quite small, she would sleep with Woody, the Jack Russell dog.

Woody didn't seem to mind at all at first. In fact, he liked the company. After a few weeks, though, it was clear that Lilly was going to be a really huge pig.

As Lilly was growing so fast, it was impossible that she could continue to share Woody's bed with him. The other thing was, she was always looking for something to eat, no matter what it was. 'I think it's time that we put Lilly in one of the pig-sheds,' said Mummy one day when she saw Lilly trying to devour one of the children's winter coats in the hallway.

Daddy set about clearing out one of the pig-sheds for Lilly. In a way, they were all sad that they had to do this, but it was the best thing for her. After all, she was a pig, and pigs always lived in proper pig-sheds, usually with other pigs. They all hoped she would be happy there.

Lilly's Adventure

One sunny afternoon when everyone was in the garden enjoying the sun and swimming in the pool, Lilly decided to go in search of food. She waddled into the house when no-one was looking and went straight to the cupboard where her food was kept. She dragged the large sack of food out and had eaten half of it before Florence found her and shouted for Mummy and Daddy to stop her eating the rest of the bag.

The girls thought it was amusing, but Mummy and Daddy were trying to be more serious about it. They found it difficult to be cross with Lilly, and everyone ended up laughing at this peculiar situation. They all helped to clear up the mess Lilly had made, and 'shooed' her out of the house. Lilly was always up to mischief. If she wasn't trying to get food or chew up clothes, she would wander off and get lost.

Missing

There was one time when Lilly disappeared and everyone was looking for her. Although she often went missing, it was usually only for a short while, and she would easily be found. This time, however, it was different - they were searching for several hours.

Florence and Isabelle looked in the gardens of all the neighbours and in unused sheds in the area, in case she had got herself locked in somewhere and couldn't get out. She was nowhere to be found.

By this time, they were getting quite worried for her safety. Eventually they had to go to bed, hoping that Lilly was somewhere safe. Maybe she would come home on her own. After all, she had done it before, although she had not stayed away for so long.

After two days of looking and finding nothing, there was a knock on the kitchen door. When Daddy opened the door, a man stood there and showed him a picture of a black pot-bellied pig! Daddy thought at once that it looked like a ransom note. He thought someone was trying to get some money from him.

In fact, it was all a bit of a misunderstanding because the man had taken a photo of Lilly so that he could show this to people to see if anyone knew who the pig belonged to.

Found

Everyone was overjoyed that Lilly had been found. The question was, where was she now? The man said to them that it wasn't far. If they could come with him, he would take them to Lilly. So, Florence, Isabelle and Daddy went with the man through the village. After several minutes he stopped at a house, and they followed him down the path, through the house, into the garden, through another building which looked like an old barn, and out into an old courtyard. And there was Lilly! They were thrilled to see her safe and well, and she was delighted to see them.

Then the man asked if they would like to stay and have a cup of tea before they took Lilly back. Daddy had a cup of tea, and the girls had some cold lemonade and biscuits. It was a scorching day so they were thankful for the drinks.

After another cup of tea and more lemonade, there was a knock on the door. To their surprise, it was Mummy. Because they had taken so long, she had come looking for them. She had cooked their dinner and was concerned about where they were. She had found them by wandering around the village to see if she could spot them anywhere, and discovered them when she heard a lot of laughter coming from the house where Lilly was.

Found

So, Mummy came in, and the man's wife brought more tea, and some cakes this time. Everyone was so happy that they had found Lilly and had got to know some new neighbours at the same time.

After about an hour, Mummy and Daddy thought it was time to go home. They thanked their new friend and his wife for looking after Lilly. It had been a very interesting experience and had ended up like a party. They took Lilly home and made sure she was put into her little pig-shed where she would be safe - until her next adventure...

www.ingramcontent.com/pod-product-compliance
Lightning Source LLC
Chambersburg PA
CBHW081358080526
44588CB00016B/2535